Happy Birthday!

Dear C V Ravindranath.

Wish you a very Happy Birthday.
May this year bring more
happiness and success in your life!

Narendra Modi

Quantum Theory of Shree Yantra

A Revelation of Siddha Kundalini Yoga

Dr. C V Ravindranath

HMCT, PDSHM, MA, MPhil, Phd (Mgmt), PhD (Philo)

ISBN 979-8-88783-526-6

ॐ MAHA TRIPURA SUNDERIYAE NAMAH:

Oh! Goddess Maha Tripura Sundari, The Governess of the Universe, the embodiment of fulfilling all my wishes, my salutations unto you. I begin my education with thy blessings and may there always be accomplishments for me.

ॐ GANAPATHAYAE NAMAH:

Curriculum Vitae of DR. C.V.Ravindranath HMCT, PDSHM, MA, MPhil, PhD (Mgmt), PhD (Philo), D. Litt (SQ).

Vision and Mission Statement of DR. C.V. Ravindranath

VISION   :– PURITY * CREATIVITY * SPIRITUALITY

MISSION   :– WISDOM * WELLNESS * WEALTH

(SARASWATI) (PARVATI)   (LAXMI)

I. Birth:

C.V.Ravindranath was born in Colombo to an affluent family of Jewellers, ISLAND GOLD HOUSE, which was that time recognized by Her Majesty Queen Elizabeth of England. He is a virgoan born on 24th August, 1954 at 9pm – Punnartham Nakshathram (VIRGO); in Ratna Hospital, Colombo, Ceylon.

II. Alumni:

1. St. Teresa's Anglo Indian Convent – Kindergarten (Baby class) – 1960.

2. St.Michael's Anglo Indian Boys' High School, Kannur – Anglo-Indian Schools Examination, Chennai (1961-1971) Madras Board of Anglo-Indian Examinations.

3. P.S.G College of Technology Coimbatore – Pre-Technical (1972-1973).

4. Birla Institute of Technology and Science (BITS) Pilani, Rajastan – 1st B Tech (Hons) – (1973-1974) (Discontinued due to extreme cold climate).

5. Hindustan Engineering College. Chennai – IIT Entrance Test coaching class – (1975-1976).

6. Institute of Hotel Management, Catering Technology and Applied Nutrition, Mumbai – HMCT, PDSHM (1976-1980).

7. Cornell University, School of Hotel Administration, USA – Hotel Sales & Marketing (1983).

8. Gemological Institute of America (GIA), USA – Fine Jewellery Sales Consultant (1991).

9. Indian Diamond Institute(IDI), Surat – Diamond – Sales (1992).

10. Indian Institute of Management (IIM), Ahmedabad – SMEP (2000).

11. Indian Institute of Kozhikode, MDP (2001).

12. Regional Engineering College & Management Studies – MDP (2002).

13. Madurai Kamaraj University, Madurai – MA & MPhil (2004-2006).

14. Indian School of Business – (ISB) Hyderabad – MDP (2007).

15. Kannur University, Dept. of Philosophy, PhD – The Prospects of Meditative Techniques in Transforming Socio – Personal Domains of Fundamentalism (2008-2013).

16. International Open University, Colombo, Honorary PhD in SQ in Business Management (2014).

17. Academy for Spiritual Scientist – Kingship Academy: Honorary Doctorate in Spirituality (2015).

GURUTHWAM

People from all walks of life appreciated the book, 'TANTRIC MANAGEMENT' in 2014. Both Spiritual Gurus and Scholars were engrossed with its formula:

Tantric Management = Creativity + Spirituality + Universality.

'Quantum Theory of Shree Yantra', adds divinity to this formula. Let me surrender this book at the feet of all my Gurus for the last 66 years. The list is too elaborate to contain in this script.

However, I can never forget OSHO, Rishi Prabhakar, Vethathiri Maharishi and Avadhoot Babaji Shivananda for initiating me into **TANTRA.** Here, **Siddha Samadhi Yoga (SSY)** and **Siddha Kundalini Yoga (SKY)** instilled in me the essence of **Vijyana Bhairava Tantra** in 1999.

On August 24, 2014, on my 60th birthday, Swami **Dr. Jagadatmananda Saraswathi of Sri Lalithambika Ashram,** Coimbatore initiated me to **Srividya upasana** by teaching me how to draw a **Shree Yantra.** Since then I had drawn more than 222 Shree Yantras and dedicated them to Devi Shethrams and friends. **Shree Yantra Mahameru** was made in 7 materials – Wood, Brass, Panchaloha, Laterite Stone, Concrete, Krishna Shila Stone and Fibre glass, which conserved cosmic energy in abundance.

This journey to divinity has the blessings of **Sri Adi–Shankaracharya** through his poetry, **'NIRVANA SHATAKAM'**, which has become my daily prayer.

My sincere gratitude to Miss. Sanita, Smt. Padmaja, Smt. Sindu and Smt. Jyoshma for helping me to bring this book unto light.

Sa Vidya Ya Vimukthaye!

🕉 *Im Hreem Shreem* 🕉

SRI ADI SHANKARACHARYA

NIRVANA SHATHAKAM – Adi Shankaracharya

This is the greatest poem ever written in this universe. It is the divine song of the Universal Consciousness.

Mano buddhya-ahankara chittani naaham
Na cha shrotrajihve na cha ghrananetre
Na cha vyoma bhoomir na tejo na vayu
Chidananda – rupah Shivoham, Shivoham!

I am not the mind, the intellect, the thought, the cognizing ego. Neither am I the ear, the tongue, the nose, the sky, the earth; fire or wind. I am Bliss Consciousness – I am Shiva.

Na cha pranasangyo na vai pancha vayuh
Na va sapta – dhatur na va Pancha kosah
Na vakpanipadam na chopastha payuh
Chidananda – rupah Shivoham, Shivoham!

I am not the breath, the fivefold vital airs, the five organs, the speech, hands or feet. I am Bliss Consciousness – I am Shiva.

Na me dvesha – ragau na me lobha – mohau
Mado naiva me naiva matsarya – bhavah
Na dharmo na chartho na kamo na mokshah
Chidananda – rupah Shivoham, Shivoham!

I have no aversion, or attachment, I don't covert nor does illusion shroud my eyes. I have no pride, attachment, duty or selfish purpose, desire or freedom for I am Bliss consciousness – I am Shiva.

Na punyam na papam na saukhyam na dukham
Na mantro na thirtham na veda na yagnah
Aham bhojanam naiva bhojyam na bhokta
Chidananda – rupah Shivoham, Shivoham!

I have transcended both virtue and sin, pleasure and pain, chants, sacred places and Vedas or sacrifices. I am neither the enjoyer (subject) or the enjoyed (object) not the enjoyment (action) – for I am Bliss consciousness – I am Shiva.

Na mrutyu na shanka na me jati – bhedah
Pita naiva me naiva mata na janmah
Na bandhur na mitram Gurur naiva shishya
Chidananda – rupah Shivoham, Shivoham!

Death cannot shake me nor can fear shake my calm, I don't know the division of caste, I have no father, mother, brother, friend, teacher or pupil and neither do I have another life for I am Bliss consciousness – I am Shiva.

Aham nirvikalpo nirakara – rupo
Vibhutvatcha sarvatra sarvendriyanam
Na Cha Sangatham Naiva Muktir Na Meyah
Chidananda-rupah Shivoham, Shivoham!

I am changeless, formless, omnipresent, I am the Lord of all sense organs. For me there is no freedom or bondage, for me there is always evenness – for I am Bliss consciousness – I am Shiva.

After a stroke in 2016, I lost my brain power; due to the congestion of 7th and 8th cranial nerve. I regained back its zeal, by reciting *'Nirvana shatakam'* daily in the morning.

It is a sure shot for a quantum leap to universalism. It will help your transcendence to the highest realms of consciousness beyond knowledge of all doctrines of every religion and all religious rituals.

You will know, who you are? Indeed, it is Self-Knowledge, Self-Realization and God-Realization.

SHIVOHAM! SHIVOHAM!! SHIVOHAM!!!

Shaktiveda Wellness Mission
23/7, First Floor, Nagaraj Reddy Building, Jigani Main Road
Anekal Taluk, Bangalore-560105
Phone: +91 99025 44185
email: swmission2007@gmail.com

www.rishidevrinarendran.org

3rd Sept 2020

Preface

I congratulate Dr. C.V. Ravindranath for the efforts he has made in writing Quantum Theory of Shree Yantra, a revelation of Sidhi Kundalini Yoga. It is considered as a guidebook for serious spiritual seekers who are determined to acquire spiritual knowledge.

India has been a major contributor to world culture since time immemorial, till the Moguls invaded and suppressed our culture.

Dr. C.V. Ravindranth is a contemplative thinker who has experienced Truth. I hear melody and completeness in his speech.

This book is an effort to place in front of a wide audience, the ancient Indian knowledge that has been with us easily for 6000 years and more.

The aim of this book is to open minds, and to provoke thoughts based on the time-tested knowledge and practices of our ancestors.

The author is placing this book and its thoughts open for readers across various schools of thought.

I appreciate Dr. C.V. Ravindranath for making this contribution towards the propagation of the richness of Indian culture.

Rishidev Narendran

Contents

Foreword   *16*

1. (i) Sarva Anandamayi (Red Bindhu)
   (ii) Sarva Siddhi Prada Chakra (Yoni – Yellow Triangle)   17

2. Sarva Raksha Chakra (8 Green Triangles)   20

3. Sarva Rogahar Chakra (10 Black Triangles)   24

4. Sarva Artha Sadhaka Chakra (10 Red Triangles)   25

5. Sarva Saubhagya Dhayaka (14 Blue Triangles)   27

6. Sarva Sankshobahana   28

7. Sarva Asha Paripuraka Chakra   30

8. Trilokya Mohana Bhupara (Three Concentric Circles
   (Time) And Three Squares (Space)   31

9. Comparative Study of Chakras in Shree Yantra in
   Siddha Kundalini Yoga   33

10. The Virtues of Shree Yantra, Siddha Kundalini Yoga
    (Sky) And Pranava Veda   38

11. Almighty Mother Nature: Worship of Shakti in
    Bharatiya Sanskriti   44

Foreword

Shree Yantra is a unique geometrical representation of the universe. Shree Yantra attracts cosmic energy from the universe and continuously spreads positive divine energy in surrounding area. Shree Yantra gives benefits of positivity, peace of mind, happiness, harmony in relationship, good health, success, wealth and several other gains.

The author of this book, Dr. C V Ravindranath with great dedication and sincerity has done a comprehensive research on Shree Yantra and conducted an elaborative study on the structure of Shree yantra, significance of each of its elements and how it attracts and spreads Cosmic Vibrant Radiance. He himself had drawn more than 222 Shree Yantras and dedicated to Devi Kshethrams, friends, family and well-wishers. The author himself have experienced Nature's benevolence, intuitive creativity, good health, success in business, peace of mind etc after Sri Vidya Upasana and Sidha Kundalini Yoga. The author wants to bring into light, the powers of our ancient wisdom and tap the resources to benefit the world by spreading Divine energy especially during this Kali Yuga.

Unlock the mystery of Shree Yantra with this book and attract abundance in your life.

Devi Bless!

15th Sept 2020   Sanita Ravindranath, BHM, MBA (USA)

Chapter 1

(i) SARVA ANANDAMAYI (Red Bindhu)
(ii) SARVA SIDDHI PRADA CHAKRA
(Yoni – Yellow Triangle)

Shree Yantra is composed of 9 triangles. Intersection of 4 triangles pointing upwards called **SHIVA** △ and 5 triangles pointing downwards called **SHAKTI** ▽. It signifies 4 Consciousness and 5 basic elements called **Pancha Bhuta**. It reflects quantum theory of life in this cosmos – **COSMIC VIBRANT RADIANCE (CVR).**

SR No	4 consciousness △ SHIVA – STATIC ENERGY	PANCHA BHUTA(5) ▽ SHAKTI – KINETIC ENERGY	Tantric Chakras	Traits	Mantra	Mudra
1	Individual consciousness	Earth (Prithvi)	Muladhara	Sexuality	Lumm	Prithvi
2	Collective consciousness	Water (Jal)	Swadisthana	Morality	Vumm	Varuna
3	Supreme consciousness	Fire (Agni)	Manipura	Austerity	Rumm	Agni
4	Universal consciousness	Air (Vayu)	Anahata	Integrity	Yamm	Apaan Vayu
5	Divine consciousness (Unexplored)	Ether (Akash)	Vissudhi	Unity	Humm	Akash/ Vayu

The fifth Divine consciousness will be evolved in the next **Satya Yuga**, to form a balance in the universe. Now corrections are being made by Mother Nature in this **Kali yuga**. In the **Shree Yantra** we have one yoni, downward pointing triangle with a red Bindhu. In the next **Shiva Shakti Maha Yantra** we will have a star in the centre with a red Bindu. Yoni the downward pointing triangle will be intersected by upward pointing triangle, thus making **5 SHIVA – Consciousness** with **5 SHAKTI – Pancha Bhuta**. ✡ **COSMIC VIBRANT RADIANCE of** ॐ **Light &** ॐ **Sound energies – PRANAVA VEDA.**

i) In Shree Yantra, the Centre Red Bindu is called **SARVA ANANDAMAYI CHAKRA** which is at **Srividya Peetam** above **Sahasrara Chakra** and **Gayatri Peetam**. It is to attain **Universality.**

Evolution and Involution of the universe take place at this **Red Point (Bindhu)**. In Quantum Physics it is called Black hole of Big Bang Theory.

ii) The **Yellow Yoni triangle (SHAKTI)** which contains the Red Bindu in Shree Yantra is called **Sarva Siddhi Prada,** which is at the **Gayatri Peetam,** below **Srividya Peetam** or **Sthanam**. It is for the removal of illusion – Maya to attain **spirituality**. These two peetams are above **Sahasrara Chakra,** at the crown of the head. The **Yellow Yoni triangle (Shakti)** is called **SARVA SIDDHI PRADA CHAKRA** – for the removal of **Illusion** and **Maya.**

Chapter 2

SARVA RAKSHA CHAKRA (8 Green Triangles)

There are 43 triangles formed inside the Shree Yantra by the intersection of 4 Shiva – Static energy triangles pointing upwards which represents **Consciousness;** with 5 Shakti – Kinetic energy triangles pointing downwards, representing **Pancha Bhutha.**

In Part I, we have already discussed 4 consciousness are (1) Individual Consciousness (2) Collective Consciousness (3) Supreme Consciousness and (4) Universal Consciousness. However, we are aware that the 5th Divine Consciousness is not evolved yet, which will intersect with the Yoni, represented by one yellow triangle in the centre, pointing downwards, Womb of the Universe; where all the manifestations take place in the Cosmos. The Five elements of Pancha Bhuta are (1) Earth (Prithvi) (2) Water (Jal) (3) Fire (Agni) (4) Air (Vayu) and (5) Ether (Akash).

Quantum Physics had experimented with the first four elements – Earth, Water, Fire and Air, but Ether is unknown to Science. Since human Divine consciousness is not developed, science is awaiting for the evolution of 5th Divine consciousness.

Tantra says the 5th Divine consciousness will be evolved in the next Satya Yuga. However, Tantra has spiritually studied the importance of Red Bindu (Black Hole) Yellow Yoni (Womb) of Cosmos.

SARVA RAKSHAKA CHAKRA AT GURUPEETAM in SAHASRARA CHAKRA

Now let us study the 8 green triangles enclosing Red Bindu and Yellow Yoni. It represents 3 Sharir (Bodies) and 5 Koshas (sheaths) as follows:

A) SHARIR – BODY:

1) Physical body – **Stula Sharir**

2) Astral body – **Sukshma Sharir**

3) Causal body – **Karana Sharir**

On death, **Sukshma Sharir** and **Karana Sharir** leave the **Stula Sharir** to transcend to Astral World (**Pithru Loka** or emotional world).

B) KOSHAS – SHEATHS which forms Etheric layers:

1) Food sheath – **Annamaya Kosha**

2) Breath sheath – **Pranamaya Kosha**

3) Mental sheath – **Manomaya Kosha**

4) Knowledge sheath – **Vijyanamaya Kosha**

5) Bliss sheath – **Anandamaya Kosha**

The Blissfulness, Mindfulness and Ecstasy are decided by the subtleness of our consciousness. **Siddha Kundalini Yoga (SKY)** can help the transcendence of Consciousness to the highest realms of subtleness. Indeed it is called Enlightenment, Self-realization, God realization or **Samadhi.**

Tantric Secret to achieve Samadhi:

Lord Sree Krishna in Bhagwad Geetha, says that our consciousness must be liberated from **Sanchitha Karma** (Past Deeds) and **Prarabda Karma** (Present Deeds).

Krishna proclaims, *'Sa Vidya Ya Vimukthaye!' – Nothing Purifies Like Knowledge!'*

Again, our Master of the Masters, Shri Adi Shankaracharya rightly says, '**Satyam Jnanam!**' – **Knowledge is Truth** in **Brahma Sutra,** a book of Meta Physics.

Vijyana Bhairava Yoga (SKY) highlights the three aspects of Yellow Yoni Triangle.

i)   Intelligent Awareness

ii) Instant Perception

iii) Intuitive Creativity

Perhaps it is the 3 Kinetic effects of 3 Devis:

i)   Saraswati (Effect of Wisdom).

ii) Parvati (Effect of Wellness).

iii) Lakshmi (Effect of Wealth).

These are the three resources of Mother Nature in abundance. But unfortunately human beings have exploited it in the name of exploration of Nature for the sake of Growth & Development.

In the next Part – 4, we shall try to understand the 10 Red triangles of **SARVA ARTHA SADHAKA Chakra** of **Shree Yantra** at **Vishuddi Chakra of Siddha Kundalini Yoga (SKY).** It deals with 10 aspects of **SKY (AKASH).**

Kindly refer my book **Tantric Management** in English & Malayalam available at Kairali Books, Thalikkavu Road, Kannur – 670001, Tel: 0497 – 2761200, Email: kairalibooksknr@gmail.com, Cell: 9447263609 (Mr. O. Ashok Kumar – MD). This book is available by online also.

Kindly do not get scared by **Siddha Kundalini Yoga (SKY),** **Vijyana Bhairava Tantra (VBT).** Both are simple and sweet, which could be practiced by a Common man on the street like me. In fact **Siddha Kundalini Yoga (SKY)** deals with activation of 10 Chakras in our Spinal Cord and Universe. Here, we just harmonize it by uniting or connecting the macrocosm and microcosm aspects of the Cosmos through meditation.

While **Vijyana Bhairava Tantra (VBT)** deals with 112 methods of meditation for different types of people with varied religious and psychological aspect and aspirations.

Chapter 3

SARVA ROGAHAR CHAKRA (10 black triangles)

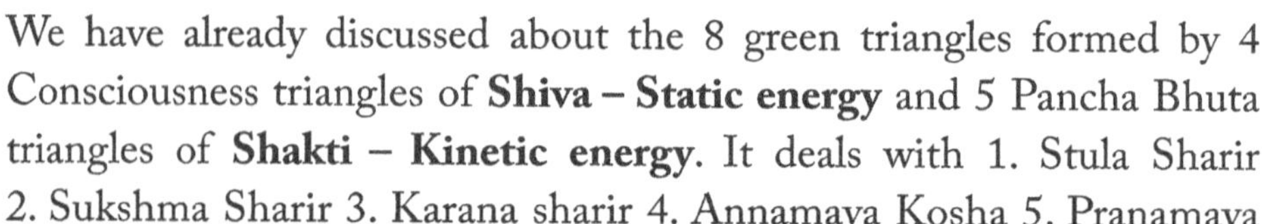

We have already discussed about the 8 green triangles formed by 4 Consciousness triangles of **Shiva – Static energy** and 5 Pancha Bhuta triangles of **Shakti – Kinetic energy**. It deals with 1. Stula Sharir 2. Sukshma Sharir 3. Karana sharir 4. Annamaya Kosha 5. Pranamaya Kosha 6. Manomaya Kosha 7. Vijyanamaya Kosha 8. Anandamaya Kosha.

Now let us study about the 10 black coloured triangles of **SARVA ROGAHAR CHAKRA** which is in align with **AGNA CHAKRA** of **Siddha Kundalini Yoga (SKY)**. It deals with 10 Devis, which are responsible of 10 Virtues.

DASA MAHA VIDYA

1. **Kali**
2. **Tara**
3. **Lalitha Tripura Sundari Shodasi**
4. **Bhuvaneswari**
5. **Bhairavi**

6. **Chinnamasta**
7. **Dhumavati**
8. **Baglamukhi**
9. **Matangi**
10. **Kamala**

Dasa Maha Vidya is followed by Dasa Maha Vidya Mantra and Sadhana. However, these 10 Devis are the avatars of **Saraswati Devi, Laxmi Devi** and **Parvati Devi**. These three kinetic energy is responsible for **Wisdom, Wealth** and **Wellness**.

Chapter 4

SARVA ARTHA SADHAKA CHAKRA
(10 Red Triangles)

In Dasa Maha Vidya, there are 10 Devis, who are responsible of 10 Virtues of 10 Vidyas: –

1	Jnanam	:	Wisdom – **'Nothing purifies like knowledge'** – **Bhagawad Geeta.**
2	Karmam	:	Deed, Action & Work promoted by Sanchita Karma, Prarabda Karma and Agami Karma **'Ma Phaleshu Kadha Chana' – Bhagawad Geeta**
3	Dharmam	:	Righteousness, Ethics, Values, Culture & Path of Religion. **'Where there is no culture, there is no Dharma' – Vyasa Maharshi**
4	Satyam	:	Truth, Honesty, Integrity **'Truth is God and it is God' – Mahatma Gandhiji**
5	Kamam	:	Passion, Lust, Love, Compassionate. **'Love is God' – Jesus Christ**
6	Artham	:	Commercial Intelligence to create wealth to the Society **'Total Choiceless Awareness is the Mother of Intelligence' – J. Krishnamurti**
7	Moksham	:	Salvation & Liberation **'Sa Vidya ya Vimuktaye!' – Lord Sri Krishna**

8	**Nirvanam**	:	Self Realization/ God Realization **'Nirvana is Shunyata (Nothingness)' – Buddha**
9	**Samadhi**	:	Superconscious state
10	**Brahmam**	:	Universalism – **'Vasudaiva Kudumbakam'** – **Bhagawad Geeta**

These 10 Red triangles are called **SARVA ARTHA SADHAKA Chakra of Shree Yantra**, which is in align with **Visuddhi Chakra**.

Chapter 5

SARVA SAUBHAGYA DHAYAKA
(14 Blue Triangles)

The 14 Blue triangles in Shree Yantra at **Anahata Chakra** in **Siddha Kundalini Yoga** (SKY) are called **SARVA SAUBHAGYA DHAYAKA Chakra** in the Shree Yantra.

It represents 7 Mantras and 7 Mudras of SKY meditation:

SR No	Mantras	Element	Mudras
1	ॐ Lam ॐ	Earth	Prithvi, Mahavira or Shivalinga Mudra
2	ॐ Vam ॐ	Water	Varuna Mudra
3	ॐ Ram ॐ	Fire	Agni Mudra
4	ॐ Yam ॐ	Air	Apaana Vayu Mudra
5	ॐ Ham ॐ	Ether	Aakasha Mudra or Vayu Mudra
6	ॐ Im ॐ	Third Eye	Praana Mudra
7	ॐ Hreem ॐ	Crown	Gyaana/ Chin /Yoga Mudra

These 7 Mantras and 7 Mudras will open up all our Chakras for optimum activation for enlightenment of our consciousness, leading us to Spirituality, Universality and Divinity.

Chapter 6

SARVA SANKSHOBAHANA

In the Part I we have explained about the 4 triangles of consciousness called **SHIVA** and 5 triangles of Pancha Bhuta called **SHAKTI**. This chart will specify the 8 Lotus petals enclosing those 9 triangles of Manifestations of universe by Mother Nature. It deals with 5 Indriyangal – sense organs and 3 Minds, which stimulates Knowledge, Memory, Intelligence, Awareness, Perception, Passion, Creativity and Actions.

- i) **5 Senses and Sense Organs**: 1. Sight – Eyes 2. Hearing – Ears 3. Smell – Nose 4. Sound / Taste – Mouth 5. Touch – Skin.
- ii) **3 Minds**: i) Conscious Mind (ii) Sub – Conscious Mind (iii) Unconscious Mind.

5 Senses + 3 Minds represent 8 Rosy Lotus petals in the Shree Yantra which is called **SARVA SANKSHOBAHANA** related to **MANIPURA CHAKRA**. In **Astanga Yoga of Patanjali:** the eight steps of **Raja Yoga**, 8 virtues are enkindled:

1	YAMA (Abstentions)	:	Truth, Non-violence, Control of sexual energy, Non stealing, Non-covetousness.
2	NIYAMA (Observances)	:	Austerities, Purity, Contentment, Surrender of Ego
3	ASANA (Steady poses)	:	Hatha and Kriya yoga for **Annamaya Kosha** (Food Sheath)
4	PRANAYAMA (Control of vital energy)	:	Breathing Exercises for **Pranamaya Kosha** (Breath Sheath)

5	**PRATYAHARA** **(Withdrawal of Sense)**	:	Non – attachment and Non Possessiveness For **Manomaya Kosha** (Mental Sheath)
6	**DHARANA** **(Concentration of Mind)**	:	To enhance Will power for **Vijyanamaya Kosha** (Knowledge Sheath)
7	**DHYANA (Meditation)**	:	Intelligent Awareness, Instant Perception and Intuitive Creativity for **Anandamaya Kosha** (Bliss Sheath)
8	**SAMADHI**	:	Superconscious state

Even Buddha advised 8 right paths to **Nirvana.**

Chapter 7

SARVA ASHA PARIPURAKA CHAKRA

Sixteen yellow Lotus petals of Shree Yantra aligned to **Swadhistana Chakra** of **Siddha Kundalini Yoga (SKY),** which represents 16 **Shodasee Mantra:**

Ka Ae E La Hreem	= 5
Ha Sa Ka Ha La Hreem	= 6
Sa Ka La Hreem, Hreem	= 5
-----	
16 petals	

It is the mantra of Srividya Upasana. Adi Shankaracharya had explained each mantra in detail. It is a sure shot mantra in Tantra for purity, eradicating possessiveness, attachment and addiction. Since **Swadhistana Chakra** is water element, it is very powerful. Because our body contains 72% water, 2/3 part of Stula Sharir. The memory power of water is excellent to transmit our spiritual aspirations. That is why water is used as **Theerth** in pooja.

According to Tantra, **Swadistana Chakra** is an ocean of **Kama – Loha – Moha = Passion – Attachment – Desires.** We could overcome them only through **Dharma. Sanatana Dharma** stands for the virtue of **MOKSHA** through **Dharma.**

Recite the **Shodasee mantra,** with ॐ **Im Hreem Shreem** ॐ in the beginning followed by **Shodasee.** It will enhance your **Wealth, Wellness** and **Wisdom,** because Im = Saraswati, Hreem = Parvati, Shreem = Wealth + ॐ Light and ॐ Sound.

Chapter 8

TRILOKYA MOHANA BHUPARA (Three Concentric Circles (TIME) and Three Squares (SPACE)

Three Concentric Circles represent **TIME – (1) PAST (2) PRESENT (3) FUTURE.** Devi for time – **KALA** is **Sri Kali Devi.** She destroys all evils and **Adharma** created by time like COVID-19 pandemic onslaught (2019), MERS (2012), SARS (2002), Spanish flu (1918). We can never avoid the evil spell of time in our lifetime. Past brings agony and sorrows, while future brings anxiety. So we have to live in the present, now here. Present is the potential with **Choiceless Intelligent Awareness, Instant Perception** and **Intuitive Creativity.**

Three Squares represent SPACE – (1) Individual Space (2) Planet Space (3) Cosmic Space. In the Universe, consciousness is created by ॐ **Light,** ॐ **Sound, Space and Time = COSMIC VIBRANT RADIANCE (CVR).**

Brahma Rishi Mayan says in his book, 'Ainthram' that **Prime Existence (Moolam)** transcends into → **Time (Kaalam)** → **Rhythm (Seelam)** → **Form (Kolam)** → **Earth (Gnalam).** Mayan views the entire cosmic phenomenon in terms of these 5 aspects. From this principle **Pancha Bhutam** is created – **Earth (Prithvi), Water (Jalam), Fire (Agni), Air (Vayu), Ether (Akash).** In **Siddha Kundalini Yoga (SKY),** this phenomenon of **Trailokya Mohana Chakra or Bhupara in Shree Yantra** is called **Muladhara Chakra,** which represents sexuality and will power.

Thus we have seen from a **Red Bindu (Dot),** called **Sarva Anandamayi,** the whole cosmos was created through **YONI** (one yellow triangle pointing downwards) of **SHAKTI** (Kinetic energy); which is formed by **4 triangles of consciousness (SHIVA)** interlaced with **5 triangles of Pancha Bhuta (SHAKTI).** Here, by the intersection of 9 triangles, 43 smaller triangles + one Red Bindu are formed, totaling to 44 Nos – 4+4 = 8 grids, as taught by Mayan's Pranava Veda. The form of Brahmam as an absolute space is 8x8 energy grid, which takes transitional forms of Brahmam into Octagon, then circle and finally it becomes a 9x9 energy grid called Manifestation, Brahmam as the material world. The process of this manifestation is from a single Red Dot (Bindu), which becomes multiple dots, then a line, then a pulse, which becomes 8X8 energy grid, then unto 9x9 energy grids. Here 8x8 grids is un-manifest and 9x9 grids is manifest. (Reference: Pranava Veda the Lost Veda).

Thus **Shree Yantra** is the **Cosmic seed (Plan)** for creation of this Universe and **Shree Yantra Mahameru, the Module of the structure of universe.**

That is why **SHREE YANTRA** is called the Queen Mother of all Yantras in this Cosmos. **'PRANAVA VEDA'** is called the King of all Vedas, because it depicts all the 64 creative divine Arts of the Universe; through **Sabda Veda (Poetry), Gandharva Veda (Music), Natya Veda (Dance), Sthapatiya Veda (Architecture and Vaastu Shastra)** and **Omkaram (Cosmology).**

To understand these divine aspects of life, we have to practice daily **Siddha Kundalini Yoga (SKY),** where Kundalini – the life force energy transcend from **Muladharam → Swadishtanam → Manipuram → Anahatam → Vissudhi → Agna → Sahasraram → Gurupeetam → Gayatri Peetam → Srividya sthanam.**

This ultimate knowledge is called **Shree Vidya** and it is attained through **Shree Vidya Upasana.** Bhagavad Geetha says: *'Sa Vidya Ya Vimukthaye!'* – **Nothing purifies like knowledge.** Ultimately, the Master of Masters, Sri Adi Shankaracharya rightly says, **'Satyam Jnanam'** – **Knowledge is TRUTH.**

Chapter 9

Comparative study of Chakras in Shree Yantra in Siddha Kundalini Yoga

Along with endocrine glands & Organs of Human Physiology

SR No	SHREE YANTRA CHAKRAS	Siddha Kundalini Yoga (SKY) CHAKRAS – Colour and Mantram	Endocrine Glands & Organs	Traits	Element
1	Sarva Anandamayi (Red Bindu)	1. Sri Vidya Sthaan ॐ Sri Vidyae Namah	1. Above the head and Gayatri Peetam	1. Universality	1. ॐLight
2	Sarva Siddhi Prada (Yellow Triangle – Yoni)	2. Gayatri Peetam ॐ Gayatriyae Namah:	2. Above the head and Gurupeetam & Sahasraram	2. Spirituality	2. ॐSound
3	Sarva Raksha (8 Green Triangles)	3. Guru Peetam – Gurupiyom Namah: Sahasraram (Violet) – ॐ Hreem ॐ	3. Pineal – Brain	3. Purity	3. Satyam (Truth)
4	Sarva Rogahar (10 Black Triangles)	4. Agna (Indigo) – ॐ Im ॐ	4. Pituitary & Hypo Thalamus. Brain, Eyes and Ears	4. Creativity	4. Jnanam (Wisdom)

5	Sarva Artha Sadhaka (10 Red Triangles)	5. Visuddhi (Blue) – ॐ Ham ॐ	5. Thyroid & Parathyroid.Throat, Mouth, Tongue	5. Unity	5. Ether (Akash)
6	Sarva Saubagyadhayaka (14 Blue Triangles)	6. Anahata (green) – ॐ Yam ॐ	6. Thymus. Heart & Lungs	6. Integrity	6. Air(Vayu)
7	Sarva Sankshobhana (8 Rosy Lotus Petals)	7. Manipuram (Yellow) – ॐ Ram ॐ	7. Pancreas & Spleen – Intestines & Liver	7. Austerity	7. Fire (Agni)
8	Sarva Asha Paripuraka (16 Yellow Lotus petals)	8. Swadisthanam (Orange) – ॐ Vam ॐ	8. Adrenal – Kidneys & Colon	8. Morality	8. Water(Jalam)
9	Three concentric circles (Time: Past, Present, Future)	9. } 10. Muladharam (Red) ॐ Lam ॐ	9. } 10. Testes & Ovaries – Penis & Vagina	9. } 10. Sexuality	9. } 10. Earth (Prithvi)
10	Trailokya Mohana Or Bhupura (3 squares – SPACE)				

SIDDHA KUNDALINI YOGA(SKY)

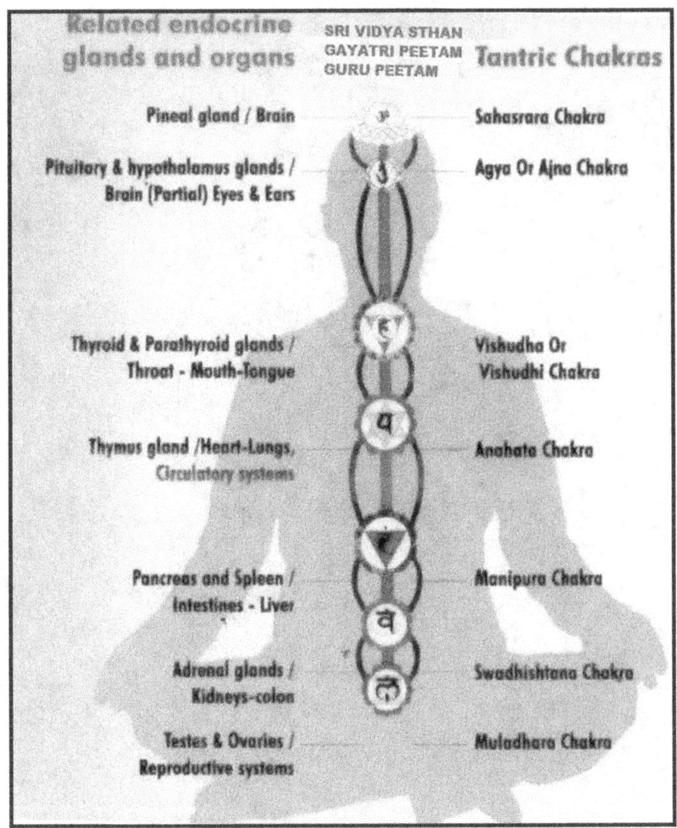

SHREE YANTRA MAHAMERU

SHREE YANTRA

The Seven Chakras

SAHASRARA CHAKRA

The seventh, highest, chakra is represented by a 1,000-petalled lotus, symbolizing the infinite.

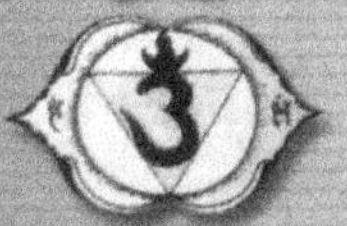

AJNA CHAKRA

Located in the middle of the forehead, the "Third Eye", as it is often called, has the mantra OM as its seed letter.

VISHUDDHA CHAKRA

As the fifth energy centre in the Astral Body, Vishuddha is located at a point corresponding to the base of the throat.

The seed mantra of this chakra is Ham.

ANAHATA CHAKRA

Use of the Anahata Chakra, or Heart Centre, as a focal point for meditation generates such pure qualities as cosmic love.

Two triangles, representing Siva and Shakti, contain the mantra Yam.

MANIPURA CHAKRA

Located at the navel, Manipura corresponds to the solar plexus in the physical body.

A downward-pointing triangle contains the mantra Ram.

SWADHISHTANA CHAKRA

The second chakra, shown with six petals, is situated along the Sushumna in the genital area.

A crescent moon contains the mantra Vam.

MULADHARA CHAKRA

The lowest chakra, located at the base of the spine, is the resting place of the dormant Kundalini (spiritual potential).

This chakra's mantra is Lam.

Chapter 10

The Virtues of Shree Yantra, Siddha Kundalini Yoga (SKY) and Pranava Veda

1. SHREE YANTRA:

Here Shiva's 4 triangles of Consciousness (1. Individual 2. Collective 3. Supreme and 4. Universal Consciousness) intersect with Shakti's 5 triangles (Pancha Bootha: Earth, Water, Fire, Air and Ether). This principle is called Manifestation of Static energy (Shiva) and Kinetic energy (Shakti).

There is an imbalance between Shiva (4) and Shakti (5). It is because the Human kind has not yet evolved the 5th virtue called **Divine Consciousness**. In **Shiva Shakti Maha Yantra**, there is a star formed in the centre, interlacing the yellow triangle called Yoni. Worship of this Yantra or its Mahameru with a star in the centre, can accelerate the transcendence of our consciousness to the highest realms of Divinity. And it can subdue all the calamities and pandemics found in the nature. Normally it is achieved during **Satya Yugam.**

2. SIDDHA KUNDALINI YOGA (SKY):

This highest realm of Divine Consciousness could be achieved through **SKY Meditation,** to transcend **Kundalini (Life force energy)** from Muladhara Chakra to **Shree Vidya Sthanam,** above our crown.

So in this comparative study, we have found there are 10 chakras both in **Shree Yantra Upasana and Siddha Kundalini Yoga (SKY),** both take our consciousness up above the sky, beyond all those dark clouds.

Even **Vijyana Bhairava Tantra** teaches us 112 methods of Meditation which Shiva (Static energy) taught to Shakti (Kinetic energy).

So in the nutshell, we can assume that the purpose of life is to attain Divinity – Divine Consciousness and Divine world. The 7th highest world the humanity can attain according to theosophical society. **Eizhezhulokam** in Malayalam means 7 Janmas in 7 worlds each, which totals up to 7 X 7= 49 janmas. The seven worlds are 1. Physical World 2. Astral World 3. Mental World 4. Intuitive World 5. Spiritual World 6. Monadic World (Monadic Intelligence) and 7. Divine World. **Shree Yantra Mahameru, Siddha Kundalini Yoga** and **Vijyana Bhairava Tantra** point towards this ultimate realms of life – **Shree Vidya Sthanam** or **Divine World** or **the abode of Shiva – Shakti.**

The secret process is to activate 10 Chakras to optimum oscillations at **c. 200 Hz** of **Gamma Waves**, which was recently discovered in hippocampus, where the functions as yet unknown. **Normally Gamma waves have 40Hz oscillations**, what might be termed its neural substrate. These Gamma waves enhance the following 10 basic traits of human kind, for the transcendence of our consciousness from sexuality to Divinity. Indeed a state of Blissfulness called **'SHIVOHAM'**, which means **I am Bliss!** In Tantra, Shiva is this bliss which Shakti is searching or longing for.

SR No	Basic Traits	Transformation after Shree Vidya Upasana and Siddha Kundalini Yoga (SKY) Meditation
1	Sexuality	1. Sex and lust are changed to **willpower.**
2	Morality	2. **Non-Possessiveness, Non-Attachments, Non-Addictions.**
3	Austerity	3. Anger & Emotions changed into **Happiness.**
4	Integrity	4. Greed, Jealousy & Envy changed into **Compassion.**
5	Unity	5. Ego and self – gratifications changed to **Peace.**
6	Creativity	6. Fear will change to **Truthfulness** and then to **Creativity.**
7	Purity	7. Ignorance blossoms unto Blissfulness.
8	Spirituality	8. Religiosity blossoms unto **Spirituality.**
9	Universality	9. Nationality blossoms unto **Universality.**
10	Divinity	10. **Cosmic Vibrant Radiance of** ॐ.

3. PRANAVA VEDA:

Brahma Rishi Mayan's PRANAVA VEDA deals with Cosmic Vibrant Radiance ॐ – both ॐ Light and ॐ Sound, which is equal to **Divine Consciousness.** It enkindles the **64 Creative Arts** as described by Bhagavad Geetha as observed in Lord Sri Krishna. These **64 Creative Arts** are 1. Architecture – Vaastu Shilpa Shastras, 2. Mediation with Adi – Vasis, 3. Bed – Covers & Pillow making, 4. Bird – training for sports, 5. Body Jewellery ornaments, 6. Cakes, bread & salad making, 7. Carpentry, 8. Children's games, 9. Cloth making, 10. Conversation & Communication skills, 11. Costumes making, 12. Crossbreeding plants & trees, 13. Crossword puzzle solving, 14. Dancing, 15. Painting and Decorating, 16. Speaking different languages and dialects, 17. Usage of Dictionary, 18. Disguise, 19. Script writing (Drama), 20. Making of Red Colour drinks, 21. Dyeing of Cloth, 22. Making Earrings of Flowers and leaves, 23. Embroidery, 24 Face & Body care, 25. Bed making,

26. Gemstone dyeing, 27. Hair care & dressing, 28. Magic tricks, 29. Hypnosis, 30. Jewel Testing, 31. Jokes Telling, 32. Jugglery, 33. Kavaca making, 34. Marionettes – Puppet show, 35. Metallurgy, 36. Mineralogy, 37. Miniature carts making, 38. Mystical Charms, 39. Respecting & glorifying others, 40. Painting & Drawing, 41. Training Parrots to speak, 42. Flower decoration on pathways, 43. Making & applying of perfumes, 44. Playing musical instruments, 45. Acting in plays, 46. Composing Poetry, 47. Making Rangoli, 48. Reciting books, 49. Making & Solving Riddles, 50. Performing Rituals & Rites, 51. Using sign language, 52. Singing, 53. Skin care, 54. Water sports, 55. Stringing flowers for garlands & beads for necklaces, 56. Tongue twisters, 57. Thread making on spinning wheel, 58. Making of crowns, Turbans, Topknots, 59. Attaining Victory, 60. Playing Veena & drums. 61. Waggery, 62. Playing water music, 63. Making bows & arrows and weapons. 64. Designing, Drawing and making Yantra.

For the Sanskrit names and more elaborate descriptions, Please refer (i) Gayatri Mahima Madhuri (cp 7, pg.100-102), (ii) Srimad Bhagavatam (10.45.35-36); (iii) Brahma – Samhita (37 tika); (iv) Bhakti – rasamitra – Sindhu (2.1.84); (v) Vrindavan Mahimamrita (11.69, 13.4); (vi) Govinda – Lilamitra (13.1140); (vii) Sadhana Amrita Chandrika (19) and (viii) Catuh – Shashthi – Kalanvitam.

Pranava Veda is a doctrine of all Creative Arts in this cosmos. It deals with

1) **Sabda Veda** – Poetry & Creative writing

2) **Gandharva Veda** – Music & Singing

3) **Natya Veda** – Dance & Drama

4) **Sthapatiya Veda** – Architecture & Vaastu Shilpa Shastras

5) **OMKARAM Cosmology** – ॐ Light and ॐ Sound

Indeed, **Pranava Veda is Creativity so Divine!**

The highest form of divine creativity is drawing, painting, designing and casting of **Shree Yantra** and its **Mahameru.** Pancha Loha,

Krishnashila granite stones, Laterite stones, Brass, wood, concrete and fiber glass are materials, we have tried with immense cosmic energy potential.

Shiva Shakti Maha Yantra is a derivation of Shree Yantra, which will be useful in Kaliyug, to balance Shiva – Shakti energies in the cosmos.

Meditation done with **Mantra, Mudra** and **Yantra** has the greatest power for the transcendence of consciousness to the highest realms of Divinity. Because it cleanses 3 Sharirs, 5 koshas and 10 chakras available in human body and mind for spiritual aspirations. Kindly refer 112 Methods of Meditations specified in Vijyana Bhairava Tantra.

BRAHMA RISHI MAYAN

Chapter 11

Almighty Mother Nature: Worship of Shakti in Bharatiya Sanskriti

Fortunately there is at least one culture in this whole world, where there is worship of female Goddess: **SANATHANA DHARMA** – A spiritual way of life, worship innumerable forms of feminine deities to obtain the benevolence of Mother Nature's virtues in abundance:

1) Wealth – **Mahalakshmi Effect – Kriya Shakti – Creativity**

2) Wellness – **Parvati Effect – Iccha Shakti – Will Power**

3) Wisdom – **Saraswati Effect – Jnana Shakti – Knowledge**

All these three important virtues of life are obtained through different energy sources: (1) **Jnanam** (Knowledge) (2) **Karmam** (Deeds) (3) **Dharmam** (Righteousness) (4) **Satyam** (Truth) (5) **Kamam** (Creativity) (6) **Artham** (Intelligence) (7) **Moksham** (Liberation) (8) **Nirvanam** (Nothingness) (9) **Samadhi** (Blissfulness) (10) **Brahmam** (Cosmic Energy).

Perhaps, way back before Vedas were found, there existed a spiritual way of living called **TANTRA,** where there was no organized religions like **Buddhism, Judaism, Christianity** and **Islam.** The last three are termed as **Abrahamic Religions** of one Grandfather called Abraham.

Indeed, **Vijyana Bhairava Tantra** will be the oldest scripture of the world written 5000 years ago. It deals with 112 meditations through **Tantra, Yantra, Mantra** and **Mudra.** Thus **Microcosm** – our body is connected with **Macrocosm** – Cosmic body, **Brahmam.** Henceforth **Shree Yantram,** the Queen Mother of all Yantrams, became the cosmic seed for all manifestation in the Cosmos. This Divine Geometric module became the primordial structure of the Universe, because it maintains **Golden Mean Ratio** in the design of Shree Yantra and Mahameru.

Tantra is a Meta Physics, which explains the quantum mechanics or quantum jump of **Static Energy (SHIVA)** and **Kinetic Energy (SHAKTI)** of the cosmos for **Manifestations.** Tantra is a quantum theory of **Shiva – Shakti**, where a vacuum, dark bluish black static energy holds all the Universes in the cosmos. Being static, it is called **SHIVA.**

Being a vacuum, the pressure exerted on it from outside by the **Static Energy (SHIVA), Kinetic Energy (SHAKTI)** is formed by the self oscillation of **Atoms.** Every atoms of each cell rotate to generate life and planets to revolve around the flaring sun, causing manifestations in this universe and life on this tiny planet Mother Earth. In **Tantra,** she is called **Maha Tripura Sundari** or **Adi Parashakti – Iccha Shakti** (Willpower), **Jnana Shakti** (Wisdom) and **Kriya Shakti** (Creativity).

Due to the continuous pressure exerted by the **Static Energy (SHIVA),** universe is on ever expanding mode called **INFINITY.** Dr. Stephen Hawking, the world renowned Physicist is right, when he said there will be a total annihilation of this cosmos, if there is a vacuum decay, which can happen at any time due to high pressure bubble moving at greater speed-velocity. **Tantra** called it **Pralayam** in the end of **Kaliyug,** where all manifestations of **Adi Parashakti** will be taken back through the **Red Bindu (Black Hole)** in the mid of **Shree Yantra.** Thus **Shiva** became **the God of Involution (Transformation)** and **Shakti, the Goddess of Evolution (Manifestation).**

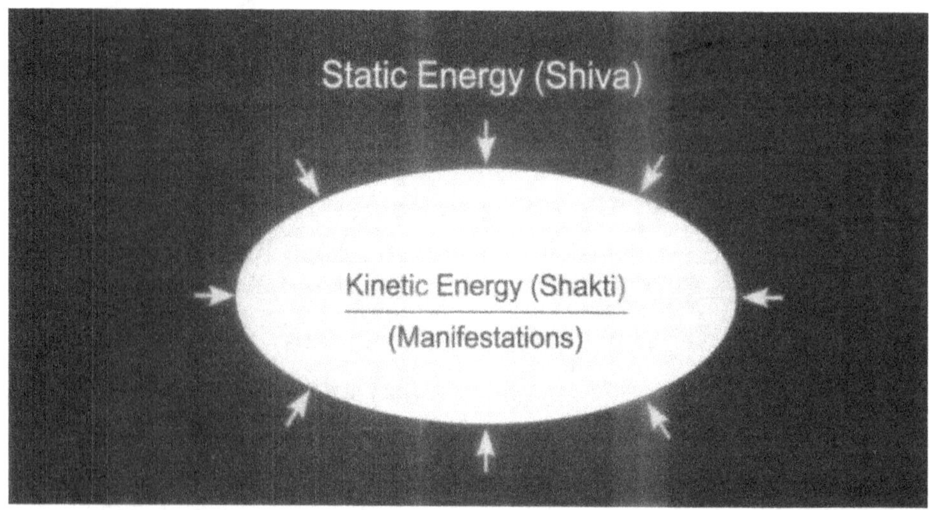

Unfortunately nobody has seen an Atom through a naked eye or through any giant telescope or very powerful microscope. Like the God, it is unseen by any living beings. But still we keep guessing a lot of the shapeless and formless energy source. Prime Existence → Time → Rhythm → Form → Earth. The free space is formed by ॐ Light and the resonance of ॐ sound is time (Mayan's Pranava Veda). **SPACE + TIME + ENERGY = CONSCIOUSNESS**

But scientists say an atom contains **Neutron, Proton** and **Electron.**

The structure of an Atom is as follows:

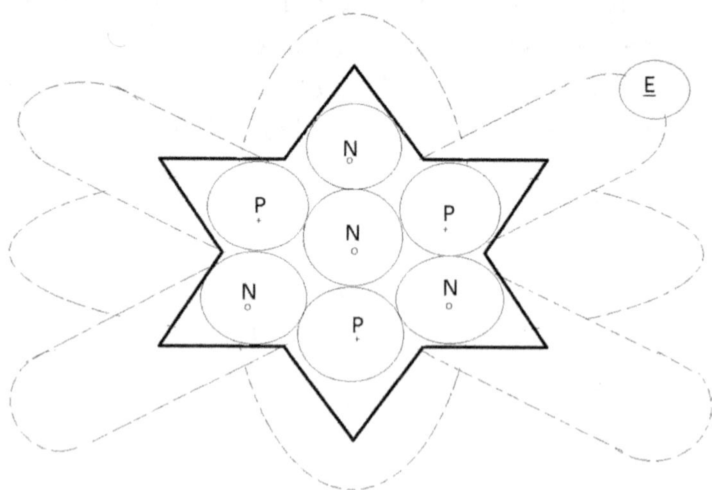

Neutrino is with zero charge (Neutral).

Proton is with Positive charge (+ve).

Neutron is with Negative charge (-ve).

Brahma Rishi Mayan says that Shiva is Static Energy (zero charged).

Vishnu is Positive Energy (+ve Charged).

Brahma is Negative Energy (-ve charged).

That is why Lord Brahma is shown outside the navel of Lord Vishnu, depicting creation. Shiva is eternal because zero represents Infinity. Science describes **Neutron** as a subatomic particle without electric charge and **Neutrino** as a stable neutral subatomic particle, which travels at the speed of light. This is the play of **Shiva – Shakti Leela.**

In **Pranava Veda,** Mayan says that the Manifestation is due to ॐ light (SHIVA) and ॐ sound (SHAKTI). Here, he stipulates that **Cosmic Vibrant Radiance = CONSCIOUSNESS;** Cosmic Radiance is ॐ Light **(SHIVA)** and Cosmic Vibrancy is ॐ sound **(SHAKTI).** When ॐ **Light passes** through particles **Space** is created and vibrations of particles create **Time** through ॐ **sound.** So consciousness is Space + Time + Energy (ॐ) and mass is created by the energy, when ॐ light + ॐ sound takes on rhythms. Albert Einstein scientifically proves that **Energy is equal to Mass x Light^2** through the formula **$E = mc^2$.** In Nataraja Statue, Shiva takes fire on the left hand and a damuroo on the right hand. Here the right brain is female (Shakti) and the left brain is male (Shiva).

In Nirvana Shathakam, Adi Shankaracharya poetically describes this phenomenon of Cosmic Energy as follows:

"Aham nirvikalpo nirakara – rupo,

Vibhutvatcha sarvatra sarvendriyanam,

Na Cha Sangatham Naiva Muktir Na Meyah,

Chidananda –rupah Shivoham, Shivoham!"

Meaning:

I am changeless, formless, omnipresent,

I am the Lord of all sense organs.

For me there is no freedom or bondage,

For me there is always evenness of balance.

For I am Bliss Consciousness – I am Shiva!

The theory of **Pranava Veda** by **Mayan** can be clearly understood by the principle of thunder & light. The light comes first, because light travels faster than sound. He says ॐ **light** and ॐ **sound** is the energy source of SHIVA – SHAKTI. Nevertheless, Neutron, Proton, Electron and Neutrino cannot be seen, even though the whole universe is created by them. Even our cells are composed by Atoms. Hence the ashes collected after cremation of our body contains Neutron, Proton and Electron.

Our Bharathiya Brahma Rishis have intuitively understood this Metaphysics and Quantum Theory, much before our scientists could experiment it in their labs, centuries later.

Meditation is the spiritual approach, while **Experimentation** is the scientific approach.

Which is the best bet? It is your Choice based on your **Intelligent Awareness, Instant Perception** and **Intuitive Creativity.** The right brain will search for Intuition, while the left brain will be only happy with scientific process.

GODDESS SARASWATI